The Children of
INDIA

THE WORLD'S CHILDREN

The Children of
INDIA

JULES HERMES

Carolrhoda Books, Inc./Minneapolis

For my family, who each in their own way have taught me to survive

Special dhanyawad to the Lafont family, Rehana and Jean Marie, Chappi Misra and Maureen Liebl, B.K. and Toshi Goswami, the Government of India Tourism Offices in New York and New Delhi, Pablo Bartholomew, Patwant Singh, Arnold Michaelis, Ted M.G. Tanen, and, most important of all, the children of India.

The publisher would like to thank Dr. Rocky Miranda, Professor of Linguistics at the University of Minnesota, for his generous assistance.

This book is available in two editions:
Library binding by Carolrhoda Books, Inc.
Soft cover by First Avenue Editions
c/o The Lerner Group
241 First Avenue North
Minneapolis, Minnesota 55401

Library of Congress Cataloging-in-Publication Data

Hermes, Jules M., 1962-

The children of India / by Jules M. Hermes.
   p. cm. — (The World's Children)
Includes index.
Summary: Introduces the variety and richness of culture in India by describing the daily lives of children from different regions and social levels.
   ISBN 0-87614-759-7 (lib. bdg.)
   ISBN 0-87614-848-8 (pbk.)
   1. Children—India—Juvenile literature. [1. India—Social life and customs.] I. Title. II. Series: World's children (Minneapolis, Minn.)
HQ799.I5H47   1993
305.23′0954—dc20   92-35103
                                                          CIP
                                                          AC

Manufactured in the United States of America

2 3 4 5 6 7 – P/JR – 00 99 98 97 96 95

Author's Note

When I was young, I remember being told I should always eat everything on my plate because there were children starving in India. I didn't understand how eating all of my supper would help solve the problem of hunger in a country thousands of miles from my home. From what I was told in school, I imagined that in India the people lay starving in the streets. I imagined endless deserts and wasteland. I imagined India must be the saddest place on earth. I wondered why anyone would want to live there. Why would anyone want to visit? So, one day I decided I would go there myself to see what I could find.

Well, I did find hordes of people living on city sidewalks. I saw the vast deserts. And I saw people starving. But I also found much more than that. I found an India where people live peacefully, their lives rich with tradition, festivals, religion, and secrets of ancient times. I found the beauty of mountains, oceans, and jungles. But most important of all, I found the beauty of the people, especially the children. Not far from the stifling cities, I met children like Nawang, a six-year-old Buddhist monk who lives in a monastery high in the Himalayan mountains. I met Noora, who lives in the great Thar Desert, Land of Princes. I made friends with children from the Araku Valley, who depend on the rich, red earth to feed them. They, and all of the children of India I encountered, welcomed me into their lives, their homes, and their hearts. They showed me the other side of India, the India filled with color and hope and happiness. And now I want to show you that India, and I hope that one day you, too, may be able to see this spectacular land.

The boys at Mayo College in Ajmer, Rajasthan, wear traditional clothing for the school's Prize Day.

Long ago, India was made up of hundreds of kingdoms ruled by *maharajahs*, or princes. The maharajahs had a great deal of power and wealth. Some maharajahs had as many as 12,000 servants and 300 wives! They lived in palaces and sent their sons to the best schools in India. The young princes arrived with their own cooks, food tasters, horsemen, and servants. The boys who now attend these fancy schools live together in hostels. These hostels are century-old houses, each with a housemother and housefather. But, for the most part, the boys look after themselves.

The princely kingdoms began to lose power by the 1850s, when most of India had come under British rule. Almost 100 years later, a great leader known as Mahatma Gandhi led the Indian people in a nonviolent movement for independence from Great Britain. As a result, India was granted its independence in 1947. Since then, the people of India have had their own government made up of elected officials. Where there were once hundreds of kingdoms, India is now made up of states, which are united under one government.

CHINA

JAMMU AND KASHMIR
Leh
Dharmsala
Amritsar
HIMACHAL PRADESH
PUNJAB
Joshimath
HARYANA
TIBET
NEPAL
SIKKIM
Gangtok
ARUNACHAL PRADESH
ASSAM
New Delhi
RAJASTHAN
UTTAR PRADESH
HIMALAYA MOUNTAINS
NAGALAND
Ajmer
Sarnath
Ganges River
MEGHALAYA
KHASI HILLS
MANIPUR
Varanasi
BIHAR
BANGLADESH
TRIPURA
GUJARAT
MADHYA PRADESH
WEST BENGAL
MIZORAM
BURMA
Daman
ORISSA
Bombay
MAHARASHTRA
BASTAR
Bay of Bengal
ANDHRA PRADESH
GOA
NORTH AMERICA
EUROPE
ASIA
India
AFRICA
KARNATAKA
Arabian Sea
TAMIL NADU
SOUTH AMERICA
KERALA
AUSTRALIA
ANTARCTICA
SRI LANKA

Princess Shivangini kisses her mother, Princess Sushma.

Shivangini is a princess who lives in a palace. Her grand-uncle was a maharajah in the state of Gujarat. Although the maharajahs' kingdoms no long-er exist, most Indians still re-spect the royal families. They are taught as part of their re-ligion that all people are born into particular groups called castes. Shivangini and her family belong to the wealthy ruler caste, the Kshatriyas. In the old days, being a member of the Kshatriya caste gave Shivangini's family the right to rule over other Indian people.

This picture of Shivangini's grandfather and granduncle was taken 50 years ago. Men no longer dress this way daily, but women continue the tradition of wearing saris. A sari is a long piece of cloth that is wrapped around the body.

It is now against the law to discriminate against people because of their caste, but most people still believe in the caste system because it is a part of their religion. Although many religions are practiced in India—including Hinduism, Buddhism, Sikhism, and Christianity—they all have one thing in common: A person's religion is the focus of a large part of his or her life.

Mandri sells roasted peanuts on the street corner in the fall and winter months. When spring arrives, she and her mother sell vegetables.

Mandri was born into the Shudra, or laborer, caste. Her father is a laborer, as was his father before him. Mandri lives in New Delhi, which became the capital of India in 1912. She is 13 years old and lives in a part of the city called New Friends Colony. Mandri likes living in New Delhi because there is always something exciting happening.

Every year on the 26th of January, Mandri and her family join thousands of Indians along the roadside to watch the Republic Day parade. People from all over India gather in their traditional costumes to celebrate India's independence. Even the Indian army rides down the avenues on their horses and camels in full costume.

Satish carries chai to nearby vendors.

India has the second largest population (about 850 million people) of any country in the world. Only China has more people. India is much smaller than China, and parts of India are very crowded. Since there are so many people, especially in the cities, there is not always enough food, shelter, or schools for everyone. Children in many families must work hard just to get by. Those who cannot afford to go to school help their parents in the fields or work in the cities.

Satish is a *chai* boy in Bombay. In Hindi, the official language of India, the word *chai* means "tea." Satish is busy from dawn to dusk selling chai. He is friendly with the other street vendors in his neighborhood. He brings them chai, and in return, they give him a piece of fresh fruit or a *chapatti*—a round, flat wheat bread—hot off the griddle.

Chapatti vendors are a common sight in India's cities.

Bombay is one of India's largest cities. It is on the coast of the Arabian Sea and has a magnificent harbor. Bombay is called the Hollywood of India because more movies are made in Bombay each year than anywhere else in the world. Because of the city's fast pace, crowded streets, and high cost of living, growing up in Bombay is a lot like growing up in a large city in other parts of the world.

The banks of the sacred river Ganges

Seetha sells deep—oil lamps—to tourists.

Seetha is a Hindu girl who lives in another of India's great cities, Varanasi, which is located on the banks of the river Ganges. Every morning at six o'clock, Seetha climbs aboard her wooden boat and paddles down the Ganges. She sells *deep*—oil lamps wrapped in flowers and paper—to worshipers and tourists who have come to Varanasi. They light the wicks and send the lamps floating down the river. In the early morning hours, the sun rises and casts its golden light on the thousands of temples that are built along the river's banks. The river Ganges is considered sacred by followers of the Hindu religion. Most Indians, about 80 percent of them, are Hindus. Hindus from all over India and other parts of the world come to the river Ganges to bathe in the holy waters and wash away their sins.

Smita performs the Bharata Natyam. The small dot of red powder on Smita's forehead is called a bindi. *Some women and girls wear the bindi as a sign of marriage. Some wear a bindi or other marks on the forehead as religious symbols. Some Indian girls wear different colored bindis to match their saris.*

Festivals and dances are an important part of life in India, especially in the south, where the beautiful Hindu dance called the Bharata Natyam is performed. Smita has been practicing the Bharata Natyam since she was a little girl. It is difficult to learn because it is made up of hundreds of movements. Each movement of Smita's feet, hands, and face tells a different part of a long and ancient story.

Harish is a Hindu from Daman, a fishing community on the coast of the Arabian Sea. All month, he has looked forward to a celebration called Gokulashtami. When the day finally arrives, the villagers tie strings of decorated clay pots across the roads. Harish and his friends form a human pyramid, with Harish at the top. Harish cracks the first pot with his head, and the pot bursts open. A sticky, sweet liquid called *ghee* splashes down, soaking everyone. Laughing and singing, they throw water on each other and proceed to the next pot, which is strung higher than the first one.

Harish and his friends form a human pyramid.

Harish bursts the clay pot at the festival Gokulashtami.

Anil's mother and sister fill baskets with dung.

Anil carries dung to his family's field.

Later in the year, in November, Hindus celebrate Diwali, the festival of lights. Diwali is celebrated for the coming of a prosperous new year. On that day, Anil, a boy from the northern state of Himachal Pradesh (Land of Snow), hurries to finish his chores. He spreads cow dung on his family's field. His mother and sister scoop up the dung and put it into big baskets. Anil carries the baskets on his head, the way most Indians carry heavy loads, and brings the dung to the fields.

When they are finished, Anil watches his mother and other women of his village decorate the outside of their old stone farmhouse with intricate patterns made from water and rice flour. These designs are made to attract Lakshmi, the goddess of wealth. Anil and his family will light oil lamps at night in hopes that Lakshmi will enter their home and bring them good fortune in the coming year. Hindus all over India decorate their homes with colorful lights, set off firecrackers, and give homemade candies and other presents to one another.

Anil's neighbor makes Diwali decorations.

19

Countryside in the Garhwal Himalayas

Deepa and her family in their courtyard

Deepa Nautiyal lives high in the Garhwal Himalayas with her family. Deepa, like most Hindus, worships hundreds of gods, but the three most important gods are Brahma, Vishnu, and Shiva. Brahma is the creator, Vishnu is the preserver, and Shiva is the destroyer. Deepa looks to these gods for all of her family's needs and makes offerings to them as a sign of her devotion.

After school each day, Deepa visits the Hindu temple in the town of Joshimath below her village. She prays for her older sister, who fell off of a mountain when she was 16. Deepa's sister is paralyzed now, and Deepa takes care of her every day. Deepa often carries her into the sunlit courtyard of their home. Deepa brushes her sister's hair, brings her tea, and keeps her company. She believes the gods will help her sister walk again.

Each morning, Deepa collects water from a nearby stream and then hikes five miles up the mountain to a forest where she gets firewood. Then she cooks breakfast in the cavelike kitchen of her home. She is making aloo *with* masala—potatoes in a spicy gravy—and huge chapattis. Her stove is a mound of red clay fueled with firewood. She uses a tiny propane stove to simmer milk for the morning chai.

Some village schools have outdoor classrooms, like this one in Sarnath, Uttar Pradesh. The students use small chalkboards as notebooks. There is a small school building, but there are no desks or chairs inside. When it's too hot to be indoors, the children sit in the shade to keep cool.

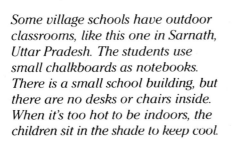

Unlike Deepa, millions of children in India cannot afford to go to school. Less than half of the population of India can read and write. With the rapidly rising population, it is difficult to educate everyone. And money is always scarce, especially for the villagers.

Some children leave their city or village homes to find work. Raju works at a restaurant on the top of the Rohtang Pass in the Himalaya Mountains. After the first snowfall, the pass closes and Raju must leave and search for another job. He is 14 years old and has no one to look after him—only an uncle who comes to take his hard-earned money from him. Raju would like to go to school, but he cannot pay for his education. So he lives the only life he knows—the life of a worker.

Raju knows how to take care of himself, and he has learned to survive on only 100 rupees, a little over $3.00, per month. (The rupee is the main unit of Indian money.) Someday, Raju says, he will get a good job, maybe driving a truck across the Rohtang Pass.

This is the Lamdon Mission school in Leh, Ladakh. One of the students, Jigmat (right), stands next to his grandmother. She escaped from Tibet to Ladakh with her children. Jigmat was the first in his family to be born in Ladakh.

Located in the highest plateaus of India's Himalayas is the district of Ladakh. In the town of Leh, the children of the Lamdon Mission school begin each day with a prayer song to the Dalai Lama. The Dalai Lama is the leader of the Tibetan people who follow the Buddhist religion. Buddhists believe they should be peaceful and never cause harm to any living thing.

Many Buddhists in Ladakh are originally from Tibet—a country to the north of India. The people there once lived in peaceful isolation high in the Himalayan mountains. But in 1959, the Chinese government succeeded in a violent, nine-year-long attempt to invade and take over Tibet. Thousands of Tibetans fled from their homeland with the Dalai Lama. More than a million Tibetans were tortured and killed, but many managed to escape across the mountains to India on foot or with long-haired oxen called yaks.

This is the Tibetan refugee school in Dharmsala. Dharmsala is where the Dalai Lama (left) now lives. Here, several Tibetan children sit along the wall at recess and listen to the words of their teacher, who is a Tibetan monk.

In preparation for a ceremony, Nawang (above) and the other young monks walk in a circle around the chortens *with two of their teachers. Chortens are like shrines, and they contain ancient texts, gold, and other precious religious items. Chortens of all sizes dot the landscape in this region.*

Nawang is six years old and is studying to become a Buddhist monk. He lives at Thiksey Monastery, which was built nearly 900 years ago. Nawang wears his cleanest red robe because, instead of lessons today, there will be a festival to celebrate the building of a new kitchen for the monastery. Men and women in silk costumes inlaid with turquoise stones will perform traditional Ladakhi songs and dances.

Nawang's family and thousands of Buddhists from the Ladakh region will come to the celebration at the monastery. The monasteries are the center of life here, and the people are proud of the traditions and beliefs that have been passed down from one generation to the next over the centuries. It is customary and considered an honor for a Buddhist family to send one son to be educated at a nearby monastery.

This statue is of Gautama Buddha, the founder of the Buddhist religion. Gautama Buddha was born in about 500 B.C. in what is now the country of Nepal, on the northeastern border of India. Nawang and the other young monks will learn about and try to lead a life like that of Gautama Buddha.

Norzing visits the Enchen Monastery in Gangtok. It is known as the Palace of Solitude. She wears a traditional Sikkimese dress, called a bhoku. Before entering the temple, Norzing rings the bell over her head.

The Gangtok market

Norzing is from Gangtok, the capital city of the state of Sikkim near the Tibetan border. Like most Sikkimese, Norzing is Buddhist. Most Sikkimese Buddhist homes have an altar room where a statue of the Buddha is kept. Norzing lights the holy butter lamps in the altar room of her family's home every day. On special occasions she and her family give offerings, such as fruits or sweets, to the Buddha.

After the quiet of the altar room, Norzing likes to visit the Gangtok market, where she and her mother buy fresh local vegetables, Sikkimese teas, and dried fish. The market is on the way to the Do-Drul Chorten. The chorten is surrounded by 108 prayer wheels and prayer flags. Buddhists string prayer flags from trees and buildings. Norzing writes her own special prayer on one of the flags and sets it to the breeze, hoping her prayers will travel with the wind.

Kuldeep and his friends are piled into a rickshah that will bring them home after a visit to the Golden Temple. The Golden Temple, which is built of marble and gold, is the holiest shrine of the Sikh people.

In keeping with the rules of the Khalsa, or "the Pure," Sikh men and boys must wear a turban and never cut the hair on their heads or faces. Like the old man in this picture, some wear the traditional belted robe and carry a long sword, or saber.

The Golden Temple in Amritsar, Punjab

Kuldeep and his friends are Sikh. Sikhism is a religion that started from Hinduism about 500 years ago. Sikhs from all over India come to worship at the Golden Temple in Amritsar and bathe in the "Pool of Nectar" that surrounds it. Ever since Kuldeep was a young child, he has followed the strict rules of his religion. For example, he always wears his hair braided and wrapped beneath his turban.

Religion is often a source of conflict in India, just as it is in other parts of the world. The Sikhs would like to create their own state in India and call it Khalistan, the Land of the Pure. But because the area they live in, the Punjab, has the best land for farming, the rest of the people of India want it to remain a part of India.

Many people, Sikhs and Hindus alike, come to the Golden Temple to worship and to listen to the musicians and singers inside the main temple. Most Indians hope that someday all Sikhs and Hindus can live together in peace.

Along with the Hindus, Buddhists, Muslims, and Sikhs, there are 18 million Christians living in India. Many live in the state of Goa. The Portuguese set up trading ports in Goa, a tiny state on the coast of the Arabian Sea. Goa was under Portuguese rule for 451 years until it was taken over by India in 1961. Now Goa's mild tropical climate and palm-fringed beaches have made it a popular vacation spot.

Dominic lives in Goa. His father is an expert fisherman, and he has taught Dominic and his brother how to spearfish. One of Dominic's favorite things to do is to fish for squid. At night, he and his friends go to the Dona Paula Pier with a lantern, a wooden pole, and a string with a hook on one end. From the pier, the boys dangle their lines on the water's surface. The light from the lantern attracts the squid. The squid are hooked and flung onto the pier. One of the boys builds a small fire, and they cook the squid right after they come out of the water.

During the day, Dominic loves to snorkel in the Arabian Sea and dive for shellfish. When he and his father go out fishing, they bring home their catch and Dominic's mother cooks it for dinner. Dominic loves his life in Goa and wants to live near the sea all of his life. He thinks he might like to be a teacher someday, so he can teach people about the sea.

Suja Rani (right) *lives in a fishing village in the state of Kerala* (below).

Like Dominic, Suja Rani lives on the west coast of India. Her village is in the state of Kerala and can be reached by boat along the backwaters of the Arabian Sea. The people of her village use Chinese fishing nets to catch fish from the waterways.

Srinivas lives on the eastern sea coast of India in the state of Andhra Pradesh. His village lies on the Bay of Bengal and is often threatened by hurricanes. During the day, Srinivas walks along the beach selling coconut juice fresh from the coconut. He carries a large knife called a machete to slice the top off of the coconut so that people can drink the juice out of the coconut with a straw. Everywhere the air smells like coconuts and flowers.

Srinivas usually sells his coconuts for two rupees (about 7 cents) each. Sometimes Srinivas can sell his coconuts for five or even seven rupees. Tourists will sometimes pay more. He gets his coconuts from the men who climb the trees daily to pluck the fruit.

Like Srinivas, four-year-old Banu lives in the state of Andhra Pradesh. However, Banu lives hundreds of miles inland from Srinivas's village and has never been to the seacoast. Banu is gathering hay for the oxen that pull the plow in the fields. Banu and all of her relatives live together in a small village called Dingriputti. There are no roads, no electricity, and no running water in the village. To reach Dingriputti, one must hike through a river, streams, and fields from the nearest road. Dingriputti is in the Araku Valley, which is known for its rich farmland and coffee plantations. Banu's home is made of red clay from the earth. Its thatched roof is made of bamboo and dried coconut leaves. Most villagers build their homes from the natural resources around them. Banu and the other children living in Dingriputti don't go to school. They learn from their parents and the other adults of the village.

Banu gathers hay.

The people of Dingriputti have their own religion and rituals. This man is the elder of the village. Every morning as the sun rises, he washes himself and then stands in silent prayer. His eyes are closed and he faces the sun. He does this to cleanse his mind, he says.

*Sumani and her mother bring their
vegetables to the village market.*

*Sumani, who has never traveled
outside of her village, reacts to
having her picture taken for the
first time.*

Many of the people who live in rural villages have very little contact with the rest of the country. Like Sumani from Bastar, they live in isolation. Sumani has never been outside of her village. There is a lot of activity in Bastar, especially during the hunting season. While the men go off into the forest to hunt wild animals, the women and girls prepare for the huge feast the village will have when the men return with their kill. To help pay for the feast, Sumani's friend Mughatti holds a wooden barrier across the road. When an auto or bus comes through, Mughatti blocks the road until the passengers throw a few rupees out the window. Mughatti, Sumani, and their friends collect the money and use it to buy special foods for the huge hunting festival.

Like Mughatti, many women from the southern states show pride in their heritage by dressing differently from other Indian women. They wear coconut oil and flowers in their hair, rings through their noses, and their own style of clothing—usually one piece of cloth wrapped at the waist or tied at the shoulder.

Trelsiolet is dressed up for a first communion celebration and the dedication of a new church. Her traditional costume is decorated with precious silver and amber stones. Some of her pieces of jewelry weigh up to ten pounds.

Trelsiolet is from Meghalaya and lives in the Khasi Hills. This region, known as the North East Frontier Agency, is very remote from the rest of India, connected only by a narrow passageway of hilly land. Trelsiolet and her family follow the traditional beliefs and lifestyle of the Khasis. They have their own language and dress. And although they are Christians, they still hold on to many of the religious practices of their ancestors.

An even more remote region of the North East Frontier Agency is the state of Mizoram. Thancchungi is a grandmother from Mizoram. She spends most of her days in her jungle garden. On the way home along the narrow path to her village, Thancchungi often meets her grandchildren. All of Thancchungi's children and grandchildren live near her in their village, Khumtang. They build their houses out of materials from the surrounding jungles and grow their own food in their gardens.

In her garden, Thancchungi grows ginger, papaya, sugarcane, and mustard leaves. There are teakwood trees and banana trees growing in the Lushai hills that surround Khumtang.

Thancchungi and her grandchildren carry food from her garden. Thancchungi remembers when Mizoram was separate from India and the Mizo people lived deep in the jungles. But in 1964, the Indian Army came into Mizoram and forced the people out of the jungles, burning down their homes. She says the children are too young to remember, but the Mizos try very hard to teach their children. The Mizos help each other. We are Mizos first, then Indians, she says.

The Rajasthanis are known for their brilliantly colored clothing. The men wear turbans to keep their heads cool. The women wear silver and ivory jewelry around their necks, ankles, and upper arms. It is possible to tell what group someone belongs to from the clothes the person wears.

The well is a hub of activity. Noora plays with the other children while her mother catches up on the latest news with her friends.

Noora's father has gone to a big camel fair in Pushkar. The Pushkar Camel Fair is held during a special period of time in November. Noora's father owns a camel that has just had a baby. He's curious to see what kind of trade he can make for the new calf.

Noora is a four-year-old who lives in Rajasthan's Thar Desert. Noora and her family are nomads. They live in a tent and move from place to place by camel, going wherever Noora's father can find work. Rajasthan is one of the hottest states of India, and water is very scarce. Noora and her mother must sometimes walk two miles with brass and clay pots stacked on their heads to collect water from the nearest well.

Most of the state of Rajasthan is desert. During the monsoon season, when the rest of India receives most of its annual rainfall, the Rajasthanis are often plagued with sandstorms. The government is trying to bring water trucks to these remote villages so that families like Noora's will be better able to survive droughts.

The Children's Day festival in New Delhi

Just as Noora and her family have learned to survive in the desert, as Raju fends for himself in the high Himalayas, and as Seetha sells oil lamps on the river Ganges, all people must learn to survive in their own way. Many Indians struggle to have enough food to eat each day, but to them, this is simply life. Their days are filled with worship, festivals, hard work, and family. And they try to live each day fulfilling their *dharma* —their duty in this lifetime. The children of India are very special people. They are strong, they are proud of their lives, and they would give everything they have to anyone who enters their home, even if it were their last cup of tea or last piece of bread. It is the Indian way.

To explain this way of life, one young Indian girl said, "If there were a god and a guest standing at the gate of my home, the guest would be asked to come in first, because a guest always comes before a god. Our gods understand these things." Then she put her hands together before her and gave the customary Hindi greeting and said, *"Namaste"*—"I bow to you."

Pronunciation note: Hindi is the official national language of India, but there are 18 major languages and hundreds of dialects spoken in India, including English. Most of the foreign words in this book are Sanskrit (an ancient language of India) or Hindi. Hindi uses a different alphabet from the one we use for English. The spellings of Hindi words in this book use our alphabet to help us know how to pronounce the Hindi words. So, you can figure out how to pronounce each word simply by sounding it out. Please note, however, that "i" is usually pronounced "ee". For example, *sari* is pronounced SAR-ee.

Glossary

aloo: potato

Bharata Natyam: a Hindu dance performed especially in the southern parts of India

bhoku: a traditional dress worn by women in the state of Sikkim

bindi: a dot of powder worn by women and girls in the center of their foreheads

Brahma: one of the three main Hindu gods, Brahma is the creator

Buddhism: the religion founded by Gautama Buddha around 500 B.C.

caste: a social class of people based on occupation. A person is born into the caste of his or her parents.

chai: tea

chapatti: a round, flat wheat bread cooked on a hot griddle

chortens: Buddhist shrines that contain precious religious objects

deep: an oil lamp

dharma: a person's duty in his or her lifetime as set out by the person's religion

Diwali: the festival of lights in November celebrated for Lakshmi and the coming of the New Year

Gautama Buddha: the founder of the Buddhist religion

ghee: a sticky, sweet liquid made from melted butter

Gokulashtami: the birthday of the Hindu god Krishna, which is celebrated in some parts of India by breaking pots filled with ghee

Hindi: the official national language of India, along with English

Hinduism: the religion followed by about 80 percent of the Indian people

Khalsa: "the Pure," members of the Sikh religion

Kshatriya: members of the wealthy, ruler Hindu caste, this is the second highest caste

Lakshmi: the Hindu goddess of good fortune

maharajah: a Hindu prince

masala: a spicy gravy

namaste: a greeting and farewell used in India to mean roughly "I bow to you"

rickshah: a two-wheeled cart pulled by a person on foot or on a bicycle

rupee: the main unit of Indian money, equal to about three cents

sari: a garment worn by Indian women. A sari is a long piece of cloth wrapped around the body.

Shiva: one of the three main Hindu gods, Shiva is the destroyer

Shudra: members of the lowest Hindu caste, mostly laborers

Sikhism: a religion founded in about A.D. 1500 that worships one god and rejects the caste system

Vishnu: one of the three main Hindu gods, Vishnu is the preserver

Index